SKIRMISHES

SKIRMISHES

CATHERINE HAYES

faber and faber

First published in 1982
by Faber and Faber Limited
3 Queen Square London WC1N 3AU
Printed in Great Britain by
Redwood Burn Ltd Trowbridge Wiltshire

All professional and amateur rights
are strictly reserved and applications
to perform must be made in advance to
Harvey Unna & Stephen Durbridge Ltd
24-32 Pottery Lane Holland Park London W11

Conditions of sale
This book is sold subject to the condition
that it shall not, by way of trade or
otherwise, be lent, re-sold, hired out or
otherwise circulated without the
publisher's prior consent in any form of
binding or cover other than that in which
it is published and without a similar
condition being imposed on the subsequent
purchaser

British Library Cataloguing in Publication
Data

Hayes, Catherine
   Skirmishes.
   I. Title
   822'.914   PR6058.A/
   ISBN 0-571-11979-4

CHARACTERS

<u>Jean</u>

<u>Rita</u>

<u>Mother</u>

SKIRMISHES was first presented at the
Liverpool Playhouse on 15 April 1981.

The cast was as follows:

<u>Jean</u>	Eileen O'Brien
<u>Rita</u>	Kate Fitzgerald
<u>Mother</u>	Frances Goodall
<u>Director</u>	Tim Fywell

The play was subsequently presented at the
Hampstead Theatre Club from 21 January 1982.

The cast was as follows:

<u>Jean</u>	Frances de la Tour
<u>Rita</u>	Gwen Taylor
<u>Mother</u>	Anna Wing
<u>Director</u>	Tim Fywell

(It is morning. <u>Mother</u> is lying in bed.
<u>Jean</u> has been up all night, and is now
sitting in an armchair looking tired and
trying to rouse herself. The curtains are
closed. Enter <u>Rita</u>, who has had a good
night's sleep. <u>Jean</u> and <u>Rita</u> look at each
other. But <u>Jean</u> turns away as if
dismissing <u>Rita</u>'s presence and
deliberately occupies herself with
something else. <u>Rita</u> looks at <u>Mother</u>, who
is perfectly still. Then, because of the
half-light, <u>Rita</u> opens the curtains. She
seems to be waiting for <u>Jean</u> to break the
silence, but <u>Jean</u> doesn't. There should
be the feeling that these two have
quarrelled the previous evening. <u>Rita</u> is
uncomfortable with <u>Jean</u>. Eventually
<u>Rita</u> speaks.)

<u>Rita</u>   Any change?

<u>Jean</u>   She's been out for a bag of chips.

              (Short pause as <u>Rita</u> decides not to
              sustain the ill feeling)

<u>Rita</u>   I meant...is she all right?

              (<u>Jean</u> doesn't answer but looks over to
              <u>Mother</u> lying in bed as if to answer the
              question)

              You know what I mean. Has anything
              happened during the night?

<u>Jean</u>   No.

              (Uncomfortable pause as <u>Rita</u> looks at
              <u>Mother</u> as if to get the answer to her
              question from there)

<u>Rita</u>   Well, she's no worse, then?

              (Again <u>Jean</u> doesn't answer but looks at
              <u>Rita</u> distastefully and succeeds in
              upsetting her slightly)

              She could've...you know...

                                                      1

Jean	No, I don't know.
Rita	She could've died.
Jean	Well, she hasn't. If she had, I'd've given you a shout. 'Ay up, Rita, your Mother's dead.' Something in that line.

(Uncomfortable pause)

Rita	Shall I give her a drink?
Jean	When she wakes up.

(Rita, for the time being, admits defeat and sits down. Jean ignores her completely. Rita is self-conscious. She looks around the room)

Rita	This place doesn't alter much.

(Jean looks briefly at the room, without interest. Rita is defeated again. There is another uncomfortable pause. Then Rita gets up as if to leave the room)

Jean	Aren't you going to stay with her now?
Rita	I want to ring Ted.
Jean	You rang him yesterday.
Rita	I want to talk to him.
Jean	If you're on ten minutes again, it's £2.76.

(Rita sits down)

I had to pay when I was at your house.

Rita	That was Ted. Anyway, it was years ago.

(Long pause. Rita feels slightly embarrassed at the memory of Jean's having to pay for the phone call and so tries to initiate conversation)

Does Mel phone you when he's away?

2

Jean	No. He doesn't need to.
	(Pause)
Rita	The children send their love.
Jean	Oh.
Rita	They're growing up.
Jean	That's not entirely unexpected.
Rita	No. (Tentatively) You still haven't...?
Jean	No.
Rita	I've never had any problems in that direction.
Jean	You've got ovaries on you like Bren guns.
	(Short pause)
Rita	There's probably an operation that'd help.
Jean	I'm all right as I am.
Rita	You'd enjoy having children.
Jean	I don't think I would. It's too much like extracting giblets.
	(Pause. Rita looks around at Mother)
Rita	If Mother is asleep, I think I will ring Ted.
Jean	Can't he manage without you?
Rita	I want to know if the children are all right.
Jean	If there was anything wrong, he'd phone. Give yourself time to be missed.
	(Short pause)
Rita	I'm sorry about last night, Jean. I

3

	was very tired.
Jean	It doesn't matter.
	(Pause)
Rita	I told Ted I'd go back tomorrow.
Jean	Tomorrow?
Rita	Yes.
Jean	Can't you stay longer than that?
Rita	No.
Jean	She might not be dead by then.
Rita	(Aware of Mother) Jean...
Jean	You'll only have to come again. Can't you make the week of it?
Rita	It's very difficult for Ted to get time off. He's taken two days' leave as it is.
Jean	Two days.
Rita	It may not sound much to you...
Jean	It doesn't.
Rita	...but it's all we can afford.
Jean	I wouldn't worry about money. You'll fill your pockets when she dies.
Rita	You'll get the house.
Jean	So I should. I live in it.
Rita	Anyway, I'm going tomorrow.
Jean	D'ye hear that, Mother? Don't linger more than forty-eight hours or we'll be back on our own again.
Rita	I don't know how she puts up with you.

4

Jean	It's not even two days, really. It's two days from when you leave your house to when you go back there. That's not two days in my terms.
Rita	It's the best I can do.
Jean	It isn't.
Rita	(Almost losing her temper) I needn't've come at all, you know. I mean, I would stay longer if I thought I could be much use. But you can cope. You've done it before. Look at when she had pneumonia.
Jean	You wouldn't come then.
Rita	The baby was sick.
Jean	Ted could've looked after it. He's had more experience with them than you have.
Rita	No mother'd leave a sick child. It doesn't matter how many children Ted had before. My child was sick and I was staying with him.

(Rita goes to Mother's bedside. She starts to push Mother's hair off her face and either put it behind her ears or clip it back. Jean watches her and is irritated) |
Jean	The bloody child's been well for months now.
Rita	(Continuing to smooth Mother's skin or nightdress or bedsheet) You can't leave them by themselves. You've got no idea... And I'm not getting anyone else in to see to them. I'm not having them upset.
Jean	If I'd rung up and told you she was dead, you'd've been on that train like a shot.
Rita	Stop talking about her as if she wasn't here.
Jean	It's all right. She doesn't know what

	we're saying. She's asleep.
Rita	She might not be.

(Jean joins Rita at the other side of the bed. When she speaks there is no response at all from Mother. Rita moves away when she realizes what Jean is doing)

| Jean | Mother? Hello. Good morning, Mother. Rita's here. Isn't that nice? She's come home for the funeral. She's come to bury you. |

| Rita | (By now away from the bed) I haven't come to bury her. |

| Jean | Well, I hope you don't intend leaving her there like that for much longer. |

| Rita | I'll bury her when she's dead. |

| Jean | (Quietly after a short pause) The doctor said yesterday it was only a matter of hours. |

| Rita | Did he? |

| Jean | Yes. He didn't think she'd see the night out. |

| Rita | You should've told me. |

| Jean | I'm telling you now. He said it was a miracle she'd lasted this long. All due to my expert nursing, of course. He made a speech about care and devotion. I think he's grateful to me for taking some of the strain off the National Health. |

| Rita | Wouldn't she be better off in a hospital? |

| Jean | She hasn't got time to get to one. |

| Rita | Jean... |

| Jean | I'm only telling you what the doctor said. He's coming back to write out the death |

6

certificate. If we need him in the
meantime, we can phone. But we won't need
him. She'll just die. She'll go off in her
sleep. She might be dead already.

Rita   (Quietly shocked and scared) She isn't,
        is she?

Jean   Come and see. That's what you're here for.

        (Rita moves over to Mother's bed. Jean
        seems nervous. They are both aware of the
        very real possibility that Mother has
        died. Rita takes her hand, listens to her
        heart and her breath. Mother is definitely
        asleep. Rita is obviously relieved)

Rita   She's all right.

        (Pause while Jean moves away and Rita
        starts to look at Mother more closely. The
        next conversation is quietly spoken)

        She looks awful. You wouldn't think it was
        the same person.

Jean   No.

Rita   Her skin's almost transparent.

Jean   I know.

Rita   It looks as if her skull's trying to grow
        out through her face.

Jean   Yes.

        (Pause)

Rita   Do you wash her?

Jean   Of course I do.

Rita   Her face doesn't look clean.

Jean   That's the colour of it. It can't be
        helped. She's got bedsores.

Rita   Bedsores?

                                                7

Jean	Yes, bedsores.
Rita	Why?
Jean	She's been lying that long.
Rita	(Becoming a little more heated) She shouldn't have bedsores.
Jean	Well, she's got them.
Rita	What have you been doing to her, Jean?
Jean	What d'ye mean?
Rita	Why has she got bedsores? You're supposed to have been looking after her.
Jean	I have been looking after her.
Rita	Haven't you got ointments to use? Don't you turn her? You're supposed to protect her from things like that.
Jean	They just developed with her lying so long.
Rita	Didn't you do anything about them?
Jean	The District Nurse had a look. She told me what to treat them with. I could do with someone here all the time to help me turn her.
Rita	She's not heavy.
Jean	She's dead weight.
Rita	You should've told me how bad she was.
Jean	I got tired of telling you.
Rita	You never said she had bedsores.
Jean	I didn't know you were interested in bedsores.
Rita	Of course I am.

Jean	I'd've sent you some photographs if only you'd've said.
Rita	(Looking at <u>Mother</u>) You've let her get into a terrible state.
Jean	So I have.
Rita	I should've known about the bedsores.
Jean	I told you about her eyesight. You didn't care.
Rita	I did care.
Jean	I told you she was going deaf. You weren't bothered.
Rita	I was.
Jean	I told you she was incontinent. You changed the subject.
Rita	You didn't tell me about the bedsores.
Jean	(Quite angry) All right. I didn't tell you about the bedsores! I didn't know you found bedsores exciting and exhilarating. I'd've made sure she got them months ago if I'd known they'd appeal to you.
Rita	The number of times you've been on the phone to me and you never once mentioned bedsores.
Jean	I never thought about them.
Rita	How could you never think about them?
Jean	I was thinking about other things. Like how the hell I was going to persuade you to come up here and give me a break. You could've brought the children with you.
Rita	What? Are you mad? Bring my children to a house like this, with a woman dying? What d'ye take me for?

Jean	She wanted to see them.
Rita	No one'd bring children here. They'd've been scared to death. They'd've had nightmares. They've never seen anything like this. You wouldn't inflict this on little ones. She smells even. Her breath smells.
Jean	They needn't've gone near her mouth.
Rita	They'd've wanted to play games in this room. Kevin would've brought his train set. Chuff, chuff, chuff. Choo, chooooooo. She'd've liked that all over the carpet, wouldn't she? I couldn't possibly've brought them. Look, oh, Peter's into everything now. He'd've been under the bed and in the bed. You need eyes everywhere with him. And once they start fighting... There would've been pandemonium. And Mother there, trying to die.
Jean	It's just that she wanted to see them so much. It's only Kevin who's ever been here. She's never seen the other two. They could've come down for the weekend.
Rita	No, they couldn't.
Jean	It's preyed on her mind. She thinks there's something wrong with her. That's why you won't bring them.
Rita	There is something wrong with her. She's had a stroke.
Jean	She thinks she's got something contagious. She thinks that's why you won't let the children near her.
Rita	My children don't like old people.
Jean	They've never seen any.
Rita	They wouldn't like them if they did see them.

10

                         (Pause. Jean becomes calmer. Rita speaks
                         quietly)

Jean   (Indicating photographs) She stares at
                         those for hours. She used to, anyway.

Rita   Ted wouldn't've let them come.

Jean   She'll never ask you for anything else.

Rita   I'm not bringing them.

Jean   If he drove down, they could be here by
                         tonight.

Rita   No.

Jean   There's nothing else she wants.

                         (Rita doesn't answer. Long pause)

                         Did you bring me those cot sheets I asked
                         you for?

Rita   No, I didn't. I forgot.

Jean   I knew you would. You expect me to
                         remember everything, though, don't you? If
                         I forgot to send one of your brats a
                         birthday card, I'd be the worst in the
                         world. I buy the damn things in bulk now.
                         Frankly, I've got them all written up for
                         the next three years. There was a sale on.
                         I do them when Mother's asleep. I've got
                         the dates ringed on my calendar. They're
                         marked off in my diary. And I don't ask
                         you for much. I'm washing sheets day in
                         and day out. My hands are scabby with soap
                         powder. I've got corrugated finger tips.
                         She's made the same as anyone else, you
                         know. She only wets sheets in the middle.
                         She doesn't do it round the edges like
                         you'd ice a cake. She hasn't got a
                         sprinkler system in there. How would you
                         like to be up to your neck in raw sewage
                         umpteen times a day? Oh, I know, you've
                         been through it all with your babies,
                         haven't you? I've tried getting her to

                                                                  11

	wear a kind of nappy, but it's not much use.
Rita	I'll wash the sheets.
Jean	Cot sheets would've been ideal.
Rita	I'll wash them!
Jean	There's no need to shout.
	(Pause. Both try to contain their anger)
Rita	(Quietly) Is this one wet?
Jean	I don't know. I never check them until she's awake. There's no point in disturbing her.
Rita	She shouldn't be lying on wet linen. It's not good for her skin.
Jean	She's not worried.
Rita	That might be how she got the bedsores.
Jean	I wash her thoroughly. I'm very particular. I use all those things you told me about.
Rita	The baby products?
Jean	Yes. I go into the chemist's and buy them. Like a real woman.
Rita	They're very good. You don't get nappy rash.
Jean	No. Well, I didn't think I would.
Rita	You have to be very careful with delicate skin.
Jean	Mother's skin's like car tyres.
Rita	(Taking Mother's hand) No, it's not.
	(Pause. Jean walks away and remains for a while with her back to Rita and Mother)

12

Jean	Aren't you phoning Ted, then?
Rita	No, I'll leave it. He's not working today. If I wait till after one o'clock, it'll be cheaper.
Jean	Will the children want to know where Mummy is?
Rita	I told them I was going away on holiday.
Jean	Was that wise?
Rita	Yes, I think so.
Jean	You'll have to take some presents back. Souvenirs. A wreath or two.
Rita	She's not dead yet.
	(Rita caresses Mother's hand. Short pause)
Jean	(Lighting a cigarette) Is she going to be cremated?
Rita	I don't know. Is she?
Jean	She never really expressed a preference.
Rita	Father wasn't cremated.
Jean	You think she'd like to snuggle down with him, then?
Rita	Yes, I think she would.
Jean	Does it matter that they were different religions? He's buried in a Catholic cemetery. He was reconciled on his deathbed, if you remember.
Rita	Can't she be buried in a Catholic cemetery?
Jean	I doubt it.
Rita	Oh, well, maybe cremation would be best.
	(Short pause as Rita continues to caress

(Mother's hand or make some other affectionate gesture. Jean watches her)

Jean   Will you want her ashes?

Rita   No. What would I do with them?

Jean   You could put them on the mantelpiece.

Rita   Why?

Jean   For an ornament. Or you could sprinkle them over your roses. Like bonemeal.

Rita   I don't think I want them.

Jean   No, neither do I.

              (Short pause. Rita is visibly upset but not crying)

Rita   I think she should be buried somewhere. I'd like to visit her grave.

Jean   We'll bury her then.

Rita   As long as that's all right with you.

Jean   Oh, it's all right with me. I rang the undertaker last week.

Rita   Why? Can you book in advance?

Jean   No. It was to get an idea of what was involved. They seem to make it very easy for you. We won't really have to do anything at all. Just give him the word.

Rita   I can't...

Jean   You can't what?

Rita   I can't imagine her dead.

Jean   I don't think she'll look much different. She's very close to it now.

Rita   I wish she'd wake up.

Jean	It's nearly over...now that you're here.
Rita	I can't take it in.
Jean	Well, I've done my best to keep you informed. I've given you an inch-by-inch account of her deterioration. I didn't think you should miss out on anything because of living so far away.
Rita	Your phone calls gave me nightmares. Ted thinks you're insane.
Jean	He would.
Rita	Mother's haunted our house for weeks.
Jean	She's been doing the same here. Isn't it strange?
Rita	There was no need for you to hold the mouthpiece to her when she was screaming. I could've done without that.
Jean	I wanted you to feel involved.
Rita	It was a heartless thing to do.
Jean	You always sounded so optimistic. She was getting worse all the time and you kept saying you were glad she was a little bit better. When I told you she'd lost the use of her left side, you said, 'Oh, well, as long as she's all right in herself.'
Rita	I must've misunderstood you.
Jean	I used to think you were drunk.
Rita	It's difficult to concentrate with the children.
Jean	You seemed to be losing the ability to comprehend anything I said.
Rita	I was very worried about her.
Jean	When I asked you when you'd be coming

15

	here, you started to tell me something about Kevin's teeth.
Rita	He's had a lot of trouble with his teeth. He's had an abscess on his top gum.
Jean	Yes, I know. You told me.
Rita	He's had to have his incisors straightened, and he needed several fillings.
Jean	Yes. You told me.
Rita	We bought him an electric toothbrush...
Jean	You told me about the electric toothbrush when I told you that Mother had begun to slobber continuously except when she was asleep.
Rita	It makes a noise when you do it properly.
Jean	She does it properly. Makes a hell of a din.
Rita	No, the toothbrush. It hums when you do the right movement. Otherwise it sizzes. It's educational.
Jean	Oh.
Rita	He loves it. He cleans his teeth all the time now. Vertical movements hum. Horizontal movements sizz.
	(Pause as Jean and Rita face each other uncomprehendingly)
Jean	Why did you put the phone down on me that time?
Rita	You were making me sick.
Jean	I was being descriptive.
Rita	There was no need.

Jean	You said you wished you were here. You claimed that you wanted to see for yourself.
Rita	You were revelling in it.
Jean	I got fed up with all the long-distance sympathy. I was tempted to make up a parcel of her droppings and post it to you.
Rita	You're not the first person who's had to look after a sick woman.
Jean	No. And you're not the first person who's opted out.
Rita	I live too far away.
Jean	You weren't expected to commute. You could've stayed here for a few weeks.
Rita	I couldn't.
Jean	A few days.
Rita	I'm here now.
Jean	Well, look after her then.
Rita	You're not going out?
Jean	I'm making myself some coffee. I've been up all night.
	(Exit Jean. Rita tries to find something to do. She straightens the bedclothes, etc. She sits in different chairs. She is obviously bored. After a lengthy pause enter Jean carrying a breakfast tray)
	Exciting, isn't it?
Rita	She's still asleep.
Jean	It goes on like this for hours. The same as when Father was dying.
Rita	You weren't much involved in that.

Jean	Neither were you.
	(Jean sits down with the tray)
Rita	Doesn't anyone come to see you?
Jean	No. Not any more.
Rita	You'd think someone'd call in. To see how she is.
Jean	Yes, you would. At least when Father was dying the people from Timber Trades Federation kept phoning up.
Rita	Oh, that lot. They probably wanted first refusal on his coffin.
Jean	Well, they showed an interest anyway.
	(Short pause)
Rita	D'you get a lot of phone calls?
Jean	No. People seem to think the phone'll disturb her. Of course, you know all about that.
Rita	What about her friends?
Jean	The few who are left feel too vulnerable.
Rita	That's easy enough to understand.
Jean	And they always have a lot of grandchildren to see to. I never realized how many people there were running around after the under-fives. They're the new aristocracy.
Rita	They are a full-time commitment.
Jean	Mainly it's just me sitting here. On my own.
Rita	Doesn't she move at all?
Jean	Hardly. At least, she hasn't during the

18

last few days. Her internal organs seem to have more or less halted. She barely shits. Once she stops slavering she'll be dead. I think there might be some sort of smell first. Aren't you going to have any breakfast?

Rita   I'm not hungry.

Jean   I eat quite a lot. It gives me something to do.

                      (Jean eats. Toast crackles. Crockery chinks. Rita is fixated, to an extent, by Jean's eating. Pause)

Rita   I do have problems of my own.

Jean   Must be awful for you.

                      (Pause. Jean continues to eat, the noise and movement emphasizing the stillness of the room. Eventually Mother moves slightly)

Rita   She's awake.

                      (Rita goes over to the bed)

                      Mother.

                      (Mother moves slightly. She gasps and slavers without really making a sound. Her distress is obvious. Rita speaks loudly and deliberately)

                      Mother, it's Rita. Are you feeling all right?

                      (Mother moves her head)

                      Is there anything you want?

Jean   She'll have a pint of mild, won't you, Mum?

Rita   Shut up. Mother, it's Rita. I've come to see you. I couldn't bring the children, but they send their love. They're sorry

	they couldn't come. They might come another time.
Jean	She can't hear you. You can say what you like.
Rita	I am saying what I like.
Jean	Are you? I'm not.
	(Mother sinks back on her pillows. Rita puts Mother's hand under the sheet)
Rita	Let her have her last few hours in peace, Jean.
Jean	Oh, I will.
	(Jean starts to eat again)
Rita	You can sit there eating at a time like this.
Jean	What d'ye expect me to do? Go on an intravenous drip?
Rita	There's no need to stuff yourself.
Jean	I'm keeping my strength up. I need it.
Rita	You've got no respect.
Jean	No, I haven't. I'm like you.
Rita	I know how to conduct myself.
Jean	Yes, you do, don't you?
Rita	What are you getting at?
Jean	You've been here five minutes and you've got the whole thing sewn up.
Rita	I've been here more than twenty-four hours.
Jean	Yes. You've spent half of it in bed and the rest on the phone.

Rita	I had a tiring journey.
Jean	I think you believe you have come for a holiday, you know.
Rita	I know what I've come for. My mother needs me.
Jean	No, she doesn't. I do.
Rita	What?
Jean	It doesn't matter to her. She knows nothing. I need someone here. She doesn't.
Rita	You can take care of yourself.
Jean	I can't. I'm going out of my mind with boredom.
Rita	That's your problem.
Jean	Look, she's asleep again. She doesn't care who's here.
Rita	I'm not staying on your account.
Jean	Mother'd want you to.
Rita	No, she wouldn't.

(Short pause)

Jean	Well, I want you to.
Rita	No.
Jean	You owe me something.
Rita	I owe you nothing. You owe me.
Jean	You've left me on my own long enough.
Rita	You're only my sister. I moved away from here years ago.
Jean	I know you did.

Rita	I've got my own life to lead.
Jean	Yes. So you have. With someone else's husband.
Rita	With my husband.
Jean	Oh. Has he stopped calling you the wrong name now?
Rita	That was a slip of the tongue.
Jean	Yes, it was.
Rita	We never think of her.
Jean	Don't we?
Rita	She's in the past. She's dead.
Jean	Like this one. But she won't stiffen.
Rita	What are you bringing this up for?
Jean	I just want to catch up on all the gossip. You don't tell me much. Sister.
Rita	It's none of your business.
Jean	Mother was always very interested in Ted's other wife. She would've liked to have met her. Wouldn't you, mum?
Rita	Don't do that.
Jean	She was anxious, you know, in case you looked like her.
Rita	She never said anything to me.
Jean	No. Well, she didn't want to worry you. (To Mother) Did you?
Rita	Why should it worry me?
Jean	Well, you know, if Ted'd married you because you were like Marian, you might've felt insecure.

22

Rita	I don't feel insecure.
Jean	Not even when he calls you Marian?
Rita	He doesn't call me Marian.
Jean	He used to. You cried once because of it.
Rita	That was a mistake. He hasn't called me it since.
Jean	Does she look like you?
Rita	I don't think so.
Jean	Who does think so?
Rita	No one. As far as I know.
Jean	Have you asked anyone?
Rita	(Short pause) Yes. I have.
Jean	Who?
Rita	I've asked her children.
Jean	Their children.
Rita	Her children.
Jean	What do they say?
Rita	They think there's a resemblance. Yes.
Jean	Oh.
Rita	A lot of people look alike.
Jean	We don't. Considering we're sisters.
Rita	Perhaps Mother had you to another man.
Jean	Yes, she could've done. She never thought much of Father.

Rita	That's just the sort of thing you would say.
Jean	Is it?
Rita	They were very close.
Jean	Only when they couldn't get out of each other's way. (To Mother) Isn't that right? Tell her. He wasn't your cup of tea, Father, was he?
Rita	She cried at his funeral.
Jean	Relief. I'll cry at hers.
Rita	Why are you telling me this?
Jean	I'll probably never see you again.
Rita	What?
Jean	You won't come back once she's dead.
Rita	Of course I will. We'll be up to see you.
Jean	If you didn't make the journey to see two of us, you're hardly likely to do it for one.
Rita	It's different when there's illness in the house. And anyway, now you'll be free to come down to us.
Jean	I don't think I want to come down to you.
Rita	Please yourself.
	(Short pause)
Jean	You'd try to turn me into some kind of unpaid babysitter.
Rita	No, we wouldn't. Don't be stupid.
Jean	It's not stupid. It's what you did last time.

Rita	I thought you liked children then.
Jean	I don't know what gave you that idea.
Rita	Well, you practically lived in the fertility clinic at the time.
Jean	Don't remind me.
Rita	Aren't you still going there?
Jean	Mel thinks I am.
Rita	And you're not?
Jean	I sacked myself a couple of weeks ago.
Rita	Why?
Jean	I got sick of being poked at and prodded at. They had me inside out. I kept picking bits up off the floor.
Rita	It's the same when you're having a baby.
Jean	I thought as much.
Rita	Surely you can put up with a bit of discomfort?
Jean	I used to come home exhausted.
Rita	It's worth it in the end.
Jean	No, it isn't. I've got nothing to show out of it.
Rita	Well, if you keep going there, they might be able to do something for you. Mightn't they?

(Pause. During the following conversation Mother's eyes open. She is obviously very ill and tired and is not fully understanding what's being said. It shouldn't look as if she's deliberately eavesdropping. Jean and Rita are not aware that she's awake)

Jean	Are you glad you've got children?
Rita	Of course I am.
Jean	No. I mean really. When you think about it.
Rita	Yes. I am glad when I think about it.
Jean	Why?
Rita	I love them.
Jean	What good does that do you?
Rita	It's better to love people, isn't it?
Jean	I don't know.
Rita	It doesn't make sense otherwise.
Jean	It doesn't make sense anyway. I don't love Mother and yet I'm stuck with her.
Rita	You do love her.
Jean	I'm sick of her.
Rita	Why are you here then? What keeps you here?
Jean	I don't know.
Rita	You wouldn't leave her. Not when she's like this.
Jean	I would if I had a good enough excuse.
Rita	Well, why don't you just go? That's all the excuse you need.
Jean	Would you stay with her if I did?
Rita	I'd stay till Mel got back.
Jean	He wouldn't do anything... What would you do if he didn't come back?
Rita	Well, I couldn't stay indefinitely. I'd have to go home some time.

Jean	How long would you stay?
Rita	I don't know. I'd try and stay till she died.
Jean	What if she started to get better?
Rita	Oh, I don't know. I'd put her in a home. I don't know. It's different when you've got children.
Jean	God.
Rita	Look, Jean, you can feel sorry for yourself all you like but don't expect me to... You wanted to live in this house. You and Mel could've bought a place of your own years ago. There was no need for you to stay here at the start. Mother didn't need you then.
Jean	She never wanted me to leave. And anyway, it would've been lonely for her on her own. Living by yourself's no joke.
Rita	You only stayed for what you could get. A house this size is worth a fortune. Ted and I are struggling. A lot of his money goes to the other kids. And what'll we get when she dies? Half of whatever's left in the bank. That's all. You'll waltz off with the other half. And this house. If I was you, Jean, I'd stay put. You're all set to make a financial killing within the next few days.
	(Mother's eyes close)
Jean	You'd've loved her more if she'd left the house between us, wouldn't you?
Rita	Yes. I would've appreciated it. I would've seen some sense in it. It would've been fair. I've got children.
Jean	I don't see what you think that entitles you to.

27

Rita   I've got responsibilities. People depend
          on me.

Jean   Why should that mean you deserve half of
          my house?

Rita   I don't see any point in this conversation,
          Jean. The business of the house has
          already been settled. You saw to that.

Jean   I didn't see to it. Mother did.

Rita   Mother, on her own, would've divided
          everything between us equally.

Jean   Would she?

Rita   Yes. She never favoured either one of us
          when we were growing up. She even used
          to dress us alike. D'ye remember those
          camel coats? She wouldn't suddenly put
          your interests in front of mine.

Jean   That's what she did.

Rita   I don't believe you.

Jean   It wasn't sudden, though. And you've only
          got yourself to blame. No one asked you
          to run off in the dead of night.
          Screeching up the alley with your tom-cat.
          Ted-cat. You weren't kicked out. You went
          of your own accord. You knew the
          consequences.

Rita   I can see your hand in this all along. I
          wrote to Mother every month. I phoned
          her when I could.

Jean   She saw you so infrequently she
          practically forgot who you were. She
          looked on your kids as total strangers.

Rita   You said she stared at their photographs.

Jean   She did.

Rita   Well, she must've known who they were,

	then, mustn't she?
Jean	I suppose she did. Once.
Rita	She wouldn't spend her time looking at people she didn't know.
Jean	She would if she had nothing else to do.
Rita	Did she ever ask you who they were?
Jean	No.
Rita	Well, then.
Jean	She never asked me anything. Only if you were coming.
Rita	If she never asked you who they were, then she must've known who they were.
Jean	I think she had an idea they were from next door.
Rita	You don't forget your own grandchildren.
Jean	If you don't see people for years on end, you forget about them. Same as anything else.
Rita	And no doubt you've helped her to forget.
Jean	Rita, I haven't helped her to do anything. She hardly ever speaks to me.
Rita	Oh, don't be stupid.
Jean	I'm not stupid. I'm the one who's here, aren't I? I know what's going on.
Rita	She must speak to you.
Jean	She doesn't.
Rita	Neither of you could cope if you didn't speak.
Jean	I didn't say I don't speak to her. I said

she doesn't speak to me.

Rita   She can't speak. She's paralysed.

Jean   Her mouth isn't.

Rita   Well, she must speak then, mustn't she?

Jean   No, she mustn't. You jump to conclusions.
       You always did.

Rita   She never had any trouble talking when I
       was here. That was the reason I left. She
       went on and on about Ted being a divorced
       man. I more or less had to marry him to
       shut her up.

Jean   She wouldn't've been so upset if he'd
       been divorced before you met him.

Rita   He'd already left his wife.

Jean   Mother thought you were the cause of it.

Rita   I wasn't.

Jean   Well, she thought you were.

Rita   I know she did. I wore my throat out
       telling her the opposite. I don't know how
       she ever had the nerve to expect me to
       come back here. In fact, she told me not
       to come back if I married him. D'you
       remember that?

Jean   Yes, I do. You virtually took her at her
       word.

Rita   She was a bigoted old cow. She never gave
       me credit for having a mind of my own. Ted
       was no different from anyone else. Divorce
       has been respectable for years.

Jean   She thought you'd let us down.

Rita   Let us down?

Jean   Not me. I didn't care. You could do what

	you liked as far as I was concerned. But she thought people'd talk.
Rita	People always talk. It's of no consequence to me.
Jean	No, well, you didn't have to sit here and listen, did you? You've always managed to make yourself scarce at the critical moment.
Rita	What Mother's friends said behind my back didn't interest me. Once they were out of earshot, as far as I was concerned, they didn't exist. Who were they, anyway? A few old cronies of Father's? Some of his timber outlets? People who bought his planks? They weren't going to run my life. And if Mother was soft enough to let them upset her, then it was her own look-out.
Jean	Why didn't you tell her that? Why didn't you say it to her face?
Rita	Why should I have?
Jean	There was no need to run away. You made her ashamed.
Rita	She was never happier than when she was ashamed. She used to look for reasons to mortify herself. She was thrilled to death when I took up with Ted. At least he was someone who excited me. He made me realize what a hemmed-in life I'd been living in this house. No wonder it gave her something to cry about.
Jean	She did cry, too.
Rita	Oh, you know nothing.
Jean	She used to confide in me.
Rita	I bet.
Jean	She did. She blamed Ted more than you.

Rita	That was decent of her.
Jean	She thought he should've known better.
Rita	Wasn't she two-faced, when you think of it, if she and Father didn't get on?
Jean	At least they stuck it out.
Rita	Is that better? To stick it out? Is that what everyone should do, stick it out?
Jean	Mother thought there was some merit in it.
Rita	Well, I don't. Would you stay with Mel if your marriage was a misery?
Jean	My marriage isn't a misery.
Rita	I said 'if'.
Jean	Mel and I aren't the same as you and Ted.
Rita	If your marriage was like Ted and Marian's, would you want it to continue?
Jean	I don't know what Ted and Marian's was like.
Rita	They didn't speak to each other. They had nothing in common. He used to stay away from home as much as he could. Would you want it to continue in those circumstances?
Jean	Yes, I would.
Rita	What if you found someone else?
Jean	I wouldn't find anyone else.
Rita	Of course you would.
Jean	Who?
Rita	Well, I don't know. You'd easily find somebody.
Jean	It took me long enough to find Mel. Where

32

	am I going to get another one?
Rita	There must be loads of men like Mel knocking around.
Jean	Where are they, then?
Rita	I don't know. I suppose they're married to women like you.
Jean	If I saw a woman like me with husband like Mel, I certainly wouldn't want to go anywhere near them.

(Short pause)

Rita	Why does Mel go away so much?
Jean	He sells floor mops and I don't wany any.
Rita	Has he got anything you do want?
Jean	He did a nice line in magnetic window cleaners once which I found very useful.
Rita	Is he coming back?
Jean	Of course he is.
Rita	How long has he been away?
Jean	A week.
Rita	Wouldn't you think he'd've got time off to be here?
Jean	No.
Rita	I think his place is with you at the moment.
Jean	He doesn't.
Rita	Has he got someone else?
Jean	No, he hasn't.
Rita	Would you know if he had?

Jean	He's not interested in anything except his bloody mops and broomsticks. Oh, and he's keen on his precious unborn child. Mel, son of Mel.
Rita	Why are you against having children?
Jean	I'm not. I just can't be bothered with all the jiggery-pokery it involves. It's like a madhouse at that clinic. One half of the women crying because they're pregnant, the other half crying because they're not. I was offered a frozen baby the last time I was there.
Rita	A whaaat?
Jean	They've got some sperm stored away in fridges. They thought I might like some, seeing as Mel's doesn't seem to work.
Rita	I never had any trouble getting pregnant.
Jean	No, well, sterility doesn't run in families, does it?
	(Mother moves erratically)
Rita	Oh, God.
Jean	It's nothing. She does that occasionally.
Rita	Does she want something?
Jean	I don't know.
Rita	Don't you go and see?
Jean	No, not any more.
Rita	D'ye just leave her when she's like that?
Jean	What else can I do?
	(Rita goes over to Mother, who continues to move)
Rita	It's all right, Mum. Calm down. Calm down.

Jean	She is calm...in herself.
Rita	Give me a hand.
	(Jean gets up)
Jean	What are you going to do?
Rita	I don't know.
	(Rita tries to hold Mother's arm to stop it jumping)
Jean	Leave her alone. She's not doing any harm.
Rita	She shouldn't be like that.
Jean	If her arm wants to jump around, let it. It mightn't be jumping tomorrow morning.
	(Rita seems startled)
	It's having its final fling. Leave it alone.
	(Rita draws back from the bed. Jean and Rita watch Mother, who continues to jump and twitch)
Rita	I can't stand it.
Jean	It's not worth getting worked up about.
Rita	It shouldn't be like that. You should be able to give her something.
Jean	Rita, there's nothing I can do to stop Mother's arm twitching. There's no reason why I should want to stop it. The arm is making unconscious natural movements which it's got no control over and which are causing no harm to anyone. And what's more, it's been doing them for quite some time now, intermittently. Don't you read my letters?
	(Rita stares at Mother, who is still twitching violently)

	I would've thought you'd be good with the elderly. They're incontinent, self-centred, difficult to communicate with and very noisy at times. Just like babies.

Rita   I can't stand old people.

Jean   The bed-ridden give me no pleasure, no matter what age they are.

Rita   Little children are different. You can love little children.

Jean   What are you supposed to do with old people? Give them poison?

Rita   I can't bear to look at her.

Jean   Well, turn away, then.

          (Rita goes and sits down)

          You're shaking, yourself.

Rita   It's enough to make you.

Jean   I'm glad you didn't come any sooner. I wouldn't't've wanted two of you on my hands.

          (Pausing, Jean looks from Mother to Rita, amused at their twitching)

Rita   You enjoy seeing her like that, don't you?

Jean   It's a distraction when you're on your own. Frankly, I've looked forward to it before now.

Rita   There's something wrong with you.

Jean   I know.

Rita   You always were odd.

Jean   No odder than you.

Rita   (Indicating the room) It wouldn't surprise me if you sold tickets for this.

36

Jean	You've no idea what it's like for me here.
Rita	I'm not deaf and blind.
Jean	You just pretend to be.
Rita	I can see what it's like.
Jean	You can't. This house is so quiet. No noise I can make seems able to fill it. I put the wireless on and the television. Anything. They don't have an impact. There doesn't seem to be an end to the silence. It hammers down.
Rita	Silence is supposed to be peaceful.
Jean	This isn't. When I die, I want it to be with noise around me. I don't want to dwindle into death like her.
Rita	I've never seen anyone die before. I only saw Father when he was already dead.

(Mother stops twitching)

Jean	Dying's overrated as a pastime. It might be great for the one who's doing it, but it's pretty dull for onlookers. She's stopped now. You can turn round.

(Short pause. Rita turns round)

Rita	D'ye think there is anything after death?
Jean	No, not for people like us.
Rita	I don't want to die. I don't want Mother to die either. I hate the thought of her moving out into darkness.
Jean	I look forward to her death. To her last breath. It's unfinished business. It needs to be settled.
Rita	She won't do you any harm if she lives.
Jean	Won't she? She'll keep me here washing

her, and wiping her, and moving her
round. She won't do you any harm because
you'll go home and forget about her again.
You'll resurrect her at Christmas and on
her birthday and perhaps when you go
abroad for a week. It won't do you any
harm if she lives. It'll just manacle me
for another few years.

Rita   You wanted the house.

Jean   I'd've got half of it anyway.

Rita   You've done me out of my rights.

Jean   Nothing in this place belongs to you.
            (Points to Mother) Though if you want
            that, you're welcome to take it.

Rita   You're not fit to be called her daughter.

Jean   Neither are you.

            (Mother's eyes open as she struggles to
            react to this conversation)

Rita   There's no feeling in you.

Jean   No, I've cleared it all out. I've
            extracted it with medicine. I've taken
            pills to keep it under control.

            (Mother starts moving violently)

Rita   She's heard you.

Jean   She hasn't.

Rita   You've upset her.

Jean   No, I haven't.

Rita   She takes notice of you.

Jean   She doesn't. She hasn't given me a thought
            for months. I mean nothing to her. I'm
            just the petroleum jelly spreader. I'm the
            thing that shakes out talc. I mean nothing.

            38

You're the one she wants. She cries for
you. She mumbles your name. She tries to
bite me sometimes when I go near her. She
only wants you.

Rita   No, she doesn't.

Jean   She does.

Rita   You're making a mistake. Or you're saying
that to get me to stay here. You're
wanting to trick me. I never got on with
her. Never. Not even when I was a child.
She always preferred you. She tried to
cover it up. She wasn't open about it,
but you were the one who shared her
secrets. I didn't. What would she want me
for now, after years of craving you?

Jean   I don't know, but she does.

              (Rita stares at Mother's violent
              twitching)

Rita   I'll have to get out. I can't breathe in
here. I'll go into the garden for some air.

Jean   Go where you like.

              (Exit Rita. Jean sighs and settles down in
              her armchair, glancing at Mother
              occasionally. Mother is still twitching.
              Jean speaks under her breath)

              Bloody cow.

              (Eventually Jean starts writing and
              crossing out on a piece of paper. Mother
              twitches, then stops. There now follows
              an eye conversation between Jean and
              Mother. Mother opens her eyes and stares
              at Jean. Jean senses something and looks
              up from the paper to stare at Mother, who
              has just closed her eyes. When Jean turns
              away Mother looks at her again. This
              happens several times, the glances
              becoming more and more hostile and darting.
              It is a wordless conversation, with

(neither <u>Mother</u> nor <u>Jean</u> completely certain that the other is taking part. It's as if they are hurling insults at each other. When they get to silent screaming pitch, enter <u>Rita</u>, who is frozen for a moment in <u>Jean</u>'s glance)

<u>Rita</u>   I'm sorry.

<u>Jean</u>   What?

<u>Rita</u>   About before.

<u>Jean</u>   Oh. It's all right.

<u>Rita</u>   It's just that when she twitches like that... I'm not used to it.

<u>Jean</u>   No.

<u>Rita</u>   I'll stay now.

      (Pause)

      Is everything all right?

<u>Jean</u>   Yes.

      (<u>Rita</u> sits near <u>Mother</u>. <u>Jean</u> picks up the paper again and starts crossing out or writing. Pause)

<u>Rita</u>   What are you doing?

<u>Jean</u>   Composing her obituary. Someone's got to do it.

<u>Rita</u>   She's not dead.

<u>Jean</u>   'Baldwin, Stephanie Jayne, 19 November, at home, peacefully; wife of Willis (deceased) and mother of Jean and Marguerite. Funeral arrangements, etc.' D'ye like it?

<u>Rita</u>   She's not dead.

<u>Jean</u>   We can easy change the date. D'ye think

	it sounds all right?
Rita	I don't know how you can do it.
Jean	Oh, Rita, don't be stupid. We may as well see to it now while our minds are clear. It's got to be done. We'll have to put something in the paper. We don't want to rush at the last minute and make a mess of it. There are people who'll need to know that she's dead. We can't ring everyone. D'ye think it sounds all right?
	(Pause)
Rita	Read it again.
Jean	'Baldwin, Stephanie Jayne, 19 November or 20 November or whatever, at home' – she will be at home – 'peacefully...'
Rita	It's not peacefully.
Jean	It's as good a word as any.
Rita	It's not peacefully.
Jean	It's what they say.
Rita	Change it.
Jean	'Suddenly'. D'ye like 'suddenly'? 'At home, suddenly...'
Rita	It won't be sudden.
Jean	'After a long illness patiently borne'?
Rita	It should be something more personal. It's too dry, what you've already got. It should be more about Mother herself.
	(Mother starts to twitch again)
Jean	'Baldwin, Stephanie Jayne, 19 November, at home, twitching...'
Rita	God.

Jean	I'm sorry.
Rita	She wouldn't've written anything like that about you.
Jean	No. I know she wouldn't.
Rita	Put 'peacefully'.
Jean	All right. D'you want 'beloved mother', 'dear mother', anything like that?
Rita	'Loving mother'.
Jean	Shall we just say 'wife of Willis (deceased)' or would you rather he was 'late'?
Rita	'Deceased'.
Jean	A lot of people write those poems. D'you like them? We could easily put one in.
Rita	Some of them are nice.
Jean	'God's garden must be beautiful, He only takes the best. He took our dear, dear mother, And laid her down to rest.'
Rita	No.
Jean	'Tears on my pillow, Ache in my heart, The day I lost you, Mum, My world fell apart.'
Rita	I don't like them.
Jean	You can write one of your own.
Rita	No.
Jean	All right. 'Baldwin, Stephanie Jayne, 19 November, at home, peacefully; wife of Willis (deceased) and loving mother of Jean and Marguerite.'

Rita	That's all right.
Jean	It's a bit bare.
Rita	I don't like the poems.
Jean	We can fill it up with where she's going to be buried. The undertaker'll be able to tell us the date straightaway. And the church is OK. Unless they have a last-minute rush.
Rita	Did she want flowers?
Jean	She never said. It's not the sort of thing you ask a sick woman.
Rita	I think there should be flowers. I know a lot of people prefer donations to charity, but I'd rather have flowers. I'd prefer flowers.
Jean	I'll bear that in mind.

(Pause. Rita stares at Mother. She is distressed but not crying)

I know you think I'm heartless, but we've had time to think about it. We don't want to arse the damn thing up.

Rita	No.
Jean	I'm in favour of anyone who wants coming to the funeral. Are you? There are people Mother wasn't too fond of, but I'm not sure who they are. I wouldn't like anyone to be left out by mistake and feel insulted. That always happens at weddings, doesn't it?

(Rita takes hold of Mother's hand and sobs. Jean looks at her. Eventually Jean goes and sits down, turning away from Rita as if trying to pretend she isn't there. After a while Rita stops sobbing. Exit Rita. After a few seconds Jean seems to smell something. She goes over to

Mother's bed)

Damn.

(Jean pulls Mother's bedsheet down and
removes her 'nappy', which she puts in
a bucket. She gets a clean towel)

That'll have to do for now.

(Jean fixes a new 'nappy' very
perfunctorily and pulls the sheet back in
place. Enter Rita with small suitcase)

Rita   I'm going home, Jean. I'm sorry. I can't
            stay.

Jean   You're running out on me again?

Rita   I can't help it.

Jean   You've got to be here.

Rita   I can't.

Jean   You're needed.

Rita   I want to go home.

Jean   God! I've done everything for you. I've
            kept her alive till you got here. Can't
            you even stay till the end?

Rita   No. I'm sorry.

Jean   I'll have to do it all on my own. There's
            everything to order. All the sausage rolls.
            I'll have to start cutting sandwiches now.
            I need you here.

Rita   I can't stand it.

Jean   I can't stand it either.

Rita   I want to go home.

Jean   What'll I say to the people? I can't ring
            them. I cry on the phone. I can't do it

                    by myself.

Rita   I want my children.

Jean   You've got to help me! I don't know how to
                   make a slab cake!

Rita   I'll try and come back. I'll bring Ted.

Jean   There's all this to do. There's everything
                   to order. Bun loaf, biscuits and cheese. I
                   don't understand about it. I won't know
                   the right ways.

Rita   I want my children.

Jean   Wait till she dies. Please wait till she
                   dies.

Rita   You can buy everything you need. Just make
                   sure there are enough serviettes. You
                   might have to borrow side plates. People
                   eat a lot in the cold weather. The old
                   ones'll want whiskey. Ted'll send you
                   money for some from us. I think you
                   should give them tea too. Give them that
                   as soon as they come in. They'll be cold.

Jean   If you don't come back, I'm not burying
                   her. She can stay here.

Rita   Ted doesn't want me to come.

Jean   Your place is here.

Rita   Ted doesn't know she's like this. He
                   thinks she's the same woman she was when
                   we went away together. She called him all
                   sorts. She said everything about him. He
                   swore he'd never let me come back here.
                   I had to fight him to come even now.

Jean   I won't put her in her grave on my own.
                   I won't. I don't care what happens. The
                   Council can have her.

Rita   Mel'll be here.

Jean	He'll stay away till it's over.
Rita	No husband'd do that.
Jean	If a daughter will, a son-in-law can.
Rita	Oh, Jean.
	(Pause. Rita is near to tears. Mother has been lying still. Now her hand and face drop on to the sheet)
Jean	Rita...she's dead.
Rita	What?
Jean	She is...she's just died.
	(They go over to the bed)
Rita	Oh.
	(Jean takes Mother's wrist)
Jean	I can't feel a pulse. She's dead.
	(Rita turns away)
Rita	Oh.
	(They are both quiet for a while, in shock. Rita sits down. Eventually Jean goes over to her after staring at Mother from a few feet away)
Jean	It's better this way.
Rita	(Very quietly) Yes.
	(They remain in an attitude of grief, Rita perhaps with her face in her hands. A long pause, during which the room is intensely quiet)
Mother	Rita!
Rita	Oh!

(Jean and Rita give a start. Mother's hand
moves as if trying to touch someone. Jean
and Rita go over to Mother's bed. Rita
takes hold of her hand)

Mum... Mum...

(Mother tries to touch Rita's face.
Eventually she falls back on the pillow,
exhausted. Rita is relieved. Silence. Long
pause as both women come to terms with
their shock. Jean moves away)

Jean   She'll do it again in a minute. Properly.

(Quite a long pause as Rita caresses
Mother's hand or face)

Rita   Something smells.

Jean   You would if you'd just... I didn't wash
              her. There didn't seem much point.

Rita   You can't leave her dirty.

Jean   The undertaker'll see to it.

Rita   I'll help you clean her.

Jean   She's better undisturbed.

Rita   We can be gentle.

Jean   We'd have to turn her. She might wake up.
              She's peaceful now.

Rita   She shouldn't be dirty.

Jean   She's not dirty. I've washed her every
              other time.

Rita   I never left my babies.

Jean   Sod your babies. How can anyone be so
              efficient with children and so inept
              with adults?

Rita   It's the bedsores, isn't it? You don't

                        want me to see the bedsores.

Jean   You can see what you like.

Rita   Have I got to do it on my own?

Jean   Don't do it at all.

Rita   I'm not leaving her like that.

Jean   She won't be refused admission to Heaven,
                you know. They won't turn her back at the
                border because her arse wants washing. I
                can remember when anyone sitting near your
                Kevin would've been gassed.

Rita   I never left them.

Jean   There's something wrong with his
                alimentary canal. That's probably why his
                teeth are so bad too. Or maybe your milk
                was off.

Rita   It's degrading.

Jean   Look, there's a man coming here in a few
                hours. We'll pay him several hundred
                pounds, and he will take her away, and
                flush her out, and hose her down, and fill
                up the holes, and remove anything that
                gives offence. She'll come back to us
                serviced and overhauled and as good as
                new. Almost. No one'd do it for her
                before, but now that there's a
                professional on the job, I'm all for
                leaving it to him. I want my money's worth.

                (Short pause. Then Rita starts to take the
                bedsheet down, turns Mother on to her side.
                Jean watches for a few seconds, then sits
                down and ignores what Rita's doing. Rita
                takes a damp flannel out of a plastic bag
                and soap, creams, etc., from the bedside
                cabinet. She cleans Mother fairly quickly
                and efficiently. When she's finished, she
                takes the flannel, towel and 'nappy'
                bucket out with her. She re-enters after
                a couple of seconds. Pause)

                        48

	I hope that's made you feel better. You'll think you're wonderful, won't you? You do it once and you're an angel of mercy. You do it every day and no one takes a blind bit of notice of you.
Rita	I know I should've come sooner... Ted hated her.
Jean	You could understand her point of view. She thought he'd make you unhappy. She thought he might run away with a younger woman and leave you with three children. He seemed practised in the art.
Rita	He was unlucky the first time. He made a bad mistake. He had no choice but to finish it.
Jean	I wish I could finish this. I've been in this room long enough. It gets on your nerves. It's too quiet. The rest of the house is worse.
Rita	Is it?
Jean	I know it's a big room, but it closes in on you. The walls are too high... I used to change the furniture around for something to do.
Rita	Did you?
Jean	Yes. It was a bit noisy, though. And I could never move the bed. It wasn't so bad at first when people came. But people get fed up with visiting the sick.
Rita	Yes, I suppose so.
Jean	You can't blame them, really.
Rita	No.
	(Pause)
Jean	The place does smell, doesn't it?

49

Rita	Actually, it smells of air freshener.
Jean	I use a lot of it. Otherwise the room stinks. You can't help it. It wants a lot of cleaning. This old furniture's heavy. I can't get the carpet up. I keep spilling things on it. When Mother's dead, I'll give it a good clean.
Rita	Yes.
	(Pause)
Jean	D'ye think I should throw the carpet out?
Rita	Well, it's pretty old, isn't it?
Jean	No, I don't think so.
Rita	You do whatever you like. Leave it all for a while after she dies, and then see how you feel.
Jean	No. I want to get rid of everything. I've seen enough of it.
Rita	Some furniture's like old friends.
Jean	This isn't.
Rita	I still think you should leave things for a while. There's no great rush.
Jean	D'you want any of it?
Rita	Well...I don't know.
Jean	I wouldn't mind. If there was something you really wanted.
Rita	You don't want to leave yourself with an empty house, do you?
Jean	I didn't mean take the lot.
Rita	No, I know you didn't. I'll think about it.
Jean	She's got some nice china.

Rita	The children might smash it up.
Jean	Oh, well, anyway, it doesn't matter.
Rita	I would like something. I'll think about it.
Jean	All right.
	(Pause as both women are alone with their thoughts)
	I don't think Mel will be back.
Rita	Don't you?
Jean	No. He's not still a door-to-door salesman, you know. He practically runs the firm. But we don't get on. I'm one of his lines that didn't sell. There was no demand.
Rita	Are you short of money?
Jean	No, I've got loads. I don't know what to do with it. He's always given me a lot since he started to earn more. I just leave it around. There's some in the desk. Quite a large amount in the bank.
Rita	You should've got a nurse in to help with Mother.
Jean	She wouldn't have anyone. I tried a couple of times. There was murder. She's been senile for ages. You can't reason with her once she gets an idea in her head. She thought they were trying to kill her.
Rita	What'll you do after all this? When the funeral's over?
Jean	I don't know. If Mel comes back, we'll try again. Probably. It'll be all right until he remembers my egglessness. Then there'll be torrid silences, and eventually he'll go off and order another thousand gross of household bleach or

51

	something. Our life's got a pattern to it, I'll give it that.
Rita	Wouldn't you adopt a child?
Jean	I would. He wants one of his own, though. Nothing soiled or second-hand. He believes in family life. (Indicating the room) Reckons it's a privilege to take part in this kind of thing.
Rita	I think men talk a lot of rubbish at times. To listen to Ted, you'd think he loved his children. The first lot. He's always comparing them with ours. Saying how much he's looking forward to seeing them. He makes a great fuss about bringing them down for the weekend. I have to clean the house out, dust the grass, prepare Cordon Bleu meals which they turn their noses up at and he goes out and leaves me with them. I don't know them. They're strangers to me. There's nothing so boring as somebody else's children. Especially when they're buggers and sods, like his are. They always finish up fighting with our three, and I get the blame for not taking their side. Sometimes I feel like telling him to gather his little monsters together and stick them back where he got them. I suppose the truth is that they resent me as much as I resent them.
Jean	They couldn't've seen much of Ted, could they?
Rita	No, they didn't. But they think they did. They think they were happier then. They can't remember, of course, but they won't admit it. I'm the villain of the piece, though. Everyone's agreed on that.
Jean	Well, Mother was very bitter. There's no point in saying she wasn't.
Rita	No.
Jean	In her day, it wasn't done. Or, at least,

52

not so openly. And she's not a forgiving
person. She never was.

(Pause)

Rita   When I look at myself now, exactly the
same as all the other wives on the estate,
I wonder what happened to the excitement
of running away with Ted. I thought I'd
written my name large. And now, I don't
know...I suppose I could run off again
with someone's husband from the next
street, but I don't think it'd work for
a second time. What else is open to me?

(Long pause as Jean doesn't answer. As
Rita starts to speak the next lines,
Mother begins to move almost imperceptibly.
She is responding to hearing Jean and Rita
speaking with more understanding of each
other)

What would you have liked to have happened
between you and Mel?

Jean   I'd've liked something deeper. Just deeper.
It's people's eyes, isn't it? Once you've
lost their eyes, it's no use.

Rita   Jean...

(Rita and Jean look at each other.
Mother's movements become more noticeable)

Look, there's...

(Mother starts to move erratically and
violently, making desperate sounds with
her mouth. They go over to her)

Mother   Rita... Rita...

(Rita takes Mother's hand)

Rita, you take everything. It's all for
you. I want you to have it. Not Jean. Make
sure Jean gets nothing. Not a thing. She
mustn't have anything. You've not to

let her.

Rita	All right. All right.
Mother	There's nothing for Jean. Not a thing.
Rita	No.
Mother	You'll have to make sure of that.
Rita	Yes.

(Mother sinks back, exhausted)

Jean	She doesn't know what she's saying.
Rita	No.
Mother	Nothing for Jean.
Rita	All right.
Mother	She took my clothes.
Jean	Oh, that again.
Rita	What?
Jean	I put her clothes in the bin.
Rita	What d'ye mean?
Jean	What I said. I was having a big clear-out. Mel'd gone off somewhere on a train, and I came back from the railway station and started clearing out the rooms.
Rita	Were they old clothes?
Jean	Some of them. They were just her clothes. She didn't want them.
Rita	Well, what did you throw them out for?
Jean	They were in the way.
Rita	A few clothes wouldn't be in the way in a house the size of this.

Jean	I couldn't move for them.
Rita	They couldn't've been in the way.
Jean	Christ, Rita, you know everything, don't you? The clothes were in the way. They'd been in the way for years. I was sick to death of them and I threw them out. Because they were in the way. They were in my way.
Rita	How could they've been?
Jean	They were.
Rita	There are dozens of cupboards and wardrobes. There's all sorts of places to store them. They couldn't've been in your way.
Jean	They were.
Rita	Did you ask her first?
Jean	No.
Rita	Why not?
Jean	Because she'd've told me to leave them alone.
Rita	You should've asked her.
Jean	They were going to go out eventually. Better sooner than later.
Rita	There might've been something she wanted to keep.
Jean	She never took any notice of them.
Rita	She knew they were here.
Jean	She wasn't falling over them every day like I was.
Rita	You might as well've ripped up all her old photographs.

Jean   Really? Well, I'll rip them up now if
you like. They're only old rubbish, fit
for the bin. Fit for setting fire to.

(Jean gets hold of the photographs of
Rita's children. Mother, who has been
listening intently, lurches forward as
much as she is able and scratches at
Jean's face)

Ah! You see what she's like?

(Rita holds Mother. Jean moves away.
She mumbles)

You see what she's like?

(Long pause as the hate between Mother
and Jean sinks in. Jean has her hand
over her face where Mother has scratched
her. Mother is seething and trying to
scratch again with pathetic, exhausted
movements. Rita is holding Mother all
the time. Eventually Rita succeeds in
soothing Mother to a certain extent.
As Jean sees Rita calming Mother,
straightening the bedclothes, etc.,
she speaks)

You'd've done the same. There were all
sorts of things cluttering up the
wardrobes. No matter what you opened,
any door and drawer, old, useless
clothes'd fall out... Mel'd gone off.
He didn't know where to. He didn't know
how long for. He didn't know what he'd
do when he got there. I couldn't go, of
course. Mother was always his trump
card... So I came home and threw the
clothes out.

(Rita leaves Mother's side and gets two
clean sheets out of a chest of drawers)

There were fur coats and shoes that hadn't
seen the light of day for years. Old
underwear, moth-eaten. Beautiful quality
originally, but faded, corroded by time.

56

You can't keep it for ever. You
wouldn't't've believed the amount. Ball
gowns from years ago. Silk. Slim-waisted.
Lovely material. Lovely. Just filling up
cupboards. No one'd seen them. Not for
years, anyway. I'd never worn things like
them. Not of that quality. They were
irreplaceable, really, but no one wanted
them. They were no use. They were from
another time... I stacked them in the
back garden. The Council got them in
the end.

(Long pause. Rita now has the clean sheets
and leaves them, folded, on Mother's bed)

Rita   She wants changing again.

Jean   She's done that on purpose.

Rita   No, she hasn't.

Jean   She waits until I've cleaned her up and
        then she does it again. She has periods
        like this when she's quite lucid.

Rita   She can't help herself. She's incontinent,
        you said.

Jean   There are times when she's all right.

Rita   She can't move her left side.

Jean   I know that. I've been telling you for
        weeks.

Rita   You should've told yourself.

Jean   You bloody hypocrite. You've done nothing,
        only cherish her memory. I've laid her out.

Rita   She's not dead.

Jean   As good as.

Rita   You're jumping the gun. You don't bury
        the living.

Jean	Not if you can stay far enough away from them, you don't. You don't need to then.
Rita	She wants changing.
Jean	I'm not doing it.
Rita	She wants to be seen to properly.
Jean	I'm not stopping you.
Rita	She should be clean. I can't bathe her on my own.
Jean	I've washed that woman for the last time.
Rita	This is no way for her to be.
Jean	I'm not washing her again.
Rita	She must've washed you hundreds of times when you were a child.
Jean	Yes, she did. And you too. So you carry on. I'll watch.
Mother	Rita.
Jean	She wants you, anyway. She's been waiting for you for weeks. Like before you were born. You were long overdue. She thought you'd never come. We were both waiting for you. And where were you? Nestled in the warm. Out of harm's way. Keeping us hanging on and hanging on. Knowing you'd arrive eventually, but not quite sure when. And she was lying there like a barrage balloon. Stuck in bed waiting for you.
Rita	I always loved my mother.
Jean	Oh, I'm sure you did.
Mother	Rita.
Rita	It wasn't always easy.

Jean	No, it wasn't.
Rita	I could wait for her to die. I never wished it on her. I didn't dig her grave in my mind.
Jean	No, you didn't. But I did. While you've been playing 'boo' and entertaining other people's children, I've been sitting here organizing a momentous event. I've had the company of black horses and shiny brass. I've had men in top hats. I've had dark net veils; I've had wreaths and sheafs and black-edged invitations. I've been doing the job properly, in the style of someone who's accustomed to silk stockings and kid-leather boots. There'll be malt whiskey and home-cured ham at this feast. It won't be a hole-in-the-corner affair, like some I could mention. Oh, God, I wish she'd hurry up and die. I want to do something else.
Rita	I'll get the water. I'll get some more soap and some clean towels. I brought oil and talcum powder with me... This cover wants changing too.
Jean	You know where everything is.
Rita	Is there a nightdress ironed?
Jean	Yes, there is.
Rita	Is there a washbowl in the bathroom?
Jean	Yes.

(Exit Rita. Mother and Jean stare at each other. Re-enter Rita, carrying a full washbowl with soap and flannel)

Rita	Come on, Mum.

(Rita puts the bowl down. She fetches baby oil and baby talc from her bag. She washes Mother's face and dries it, after propping her up on her pillow. She starts to comb

Mother's hair)

I don't think she's got the strength for this.

(Rita looks at Mother's face. She pushes her hair back and holds one of her hands tightly. Mother is lying back against the pillows. Silence. Mother dies. Her tongue protrudes from her mouth. Jean, in the meantime, has turned away and does not witness Mother's death. Rita pauses for a moment)

Jean, she's dead.

(Jean turns round. Jean and Rita look at each other)

She's dead. (More quietly) She's dead.

(Rita grips Mother's hand again and starts to cry slowly and softly. She puts her arms round Mother's shoulders and rocks gently to and fro. Jean watches this for a while)

Jean   (Quietly) She's dead.

(Eventually Jean sits down, very silently and very upset. After a long pause Rita gets up from the bed, lays Mother's head against the pillows and puts her hands under the sheets. She goes over to Jean)

Rita   Jean...

Jean   (Very quietly, almost haunted) So this is what it's like.

(Rita kneels at Jean's chair. She touches Jean's arm. She needs physical comfort)

Rita   Jean.

Jean   This is what it's come to. This is what I wanted.

(Pause)

Is there anything else?

(Rita tries to answer but succeeds only
in making an inadequate shrugging gesture.
Jean goes out of the room, leaving Rita
alone with Mother's body)